8846
The Sure Thing

Steve Bradley
AR B.L.: 3.6
Points: 0.5   UG

D1005948

MEDIA CENTER
SANTA ANA HIGH SCHOOL
520 W. Walnut Street
Santa Ana, Calif, 92701

The SURE THING

The **SURE THING**

Steve Bradley

GLOBE FEARON

Pearson Learning Group

FASTBACK® SPORTS BOOKS

Cover photographer: Richard Hutchings

Copyright © 1985 Pearson Education, Inc., publishing as Globe Fe
imprint of Pearson Learning Group, 299 Jefferson Road, Parsippan
07054. All rights reserved. No part of this book may be reproduced
transmitted in any form or by any means, electronic, or mechanical
photocopying, recording, or by any other information storage and r
system, without permission in writing from the publisher. For inform
regarding permission(s), write to Rights and Permissions Departme

ISBN 0-8224-6497-7

Printed in the United Stated of America
8 9 10 11 12 13   05 04 03 02

1-800-321-3106
www.pearsonlearning.com

There was a faraway look in jockey Carmen Solar's eyes, as she stood beside the rail of the racetrack. She was a small and beautiful young woman with large dark eyes and short black hair.

As she watched Fast Dancer run around the racetrack, she dreamed of success.

"He's the fastest thing on four feet," said Carmen's agent, Sam Martin, who stood at the rail beside her.

"I wish I could ride him in the Sullivan Stakes tomorrow," Carmen said, her eyes shining. "I really do."

"Maybe you will get to ride him someday," Sam said.

Carmen's thoughts drifted back in time as she continued to watch Fast Dancer run.

She thought about her first days at the racetrack as a stable girl. For a long time, she had cleared stables and done all the other dirty work at the track. Then she became a groom. She remembered how she had groomed all the race horses until their coats were bright and felt as soft as silk.

Then she moved up and became an exercise girl. And she had loved all those early mornings alone on the track with just the horse she was riding to keep her company.

Now I am a jockey, she thought. *And someday I'll be the best jockey in the whole country. Maybe in the whole world.*

"One minute and three-fifths seconds," Sam said, as he looked down at the stop-watch in his hand. "That's the best time Fast Dancer has ever made. It's no wonder that he's the favorite in the Sullivan Stakes tomorrow. I'd say he's sure to win."

"I wouldn't," a voice behind them said.

Carmen and Sam turned around to find Dan Blair standing in back of them.

"Good morning, Mr. Blair," Sam said, smiling. "You know Carmen Solar, I believe."

"I do, yes." Blair shook Carmen's hand. "As a matter of fact, it's Miss Solar I came out to the track to see this morning." Blair cleared his throat. "Miss Solar, I would like you to ride my horse, Whirlwind, in the Sullivan Stakes race tomorrow."

Carmen was surprised. She looked at Sam, saw his happy smile, and then smiled herself. "I'd very much like to ride Whirlwind for you, Mr. Blair. I'd like to thank you for having faith in me, and giving me the chance to ride a fine horse like Whirlwind."

"I think you're a very good rider," Blair said. "With you riding him, I think Whirlwind has a good chance of taking the race away from Fast Dancer. I'll work out the business details of your ride with Mr. Martin. Good luck on Whirlwind tomorrow, Miss Solar."

"Thank you, Mr. Blair." Carmen said good-bye to Sam, and then made her way toward the stables. Suddenly, she started running.

When she came to Whirlwind's stall, she reached out and patted the black horse's neck. "Tomorrow," she whispered. "Tomorrow, it's going to be you and me against the world, Whirlwind. Tomorrow, we're going to win the Sullivan Stakes! That's a promise!"

Carmen was still patting Whirlwind's neck, when Sam Martin walked over.

"Oh, Sam!" she cried. "I'm so happy. Why didn't you tell me Mr. Blair was thinking of offering me a mount in the Sullivan tomorrow."

"Because I didn't want to get your hopes up in case it didn't come through. Mr. Blair told me yesterday he was looking for a jockey for Whirlwind and he was thinking of asking you," Sam said.

"Why isn't Mr. Blair's regular jockey riding Whirlwind tomorrow?" Carmen asked.

"Dennis Farrell had an accident at home yesterday. He burned both of his hands. He'll be out of action for several weeks. I heard that Mr. Blair had tried to hire several other jockeys, but all of them already had mounts to ride tomorrow. So he picked you."

"Then I wasn't his first choice to ride Whirlwind."

"No, you weren't. But don't let that fact worry you. He wouldn't have asked you at all if he didn't think you could do a good job. He's pretty sure—and so am I—that you'll finish in the money tomorrow."

"In the money," Carmen repeated. She

shook her head. "I don't want to just finish in the money, Sam. Whirlwind and I aren't going to settle for second or third place. We're going to *win* the Sullivan Stakes!"

Later that day, as Carmen was leaving the racetrack, a car pulled up in front of her and a tall man got out.

"Miss Solar," the man said, "I'd like to talk to you for a minute."

"I'm afraid I'm in a hurry, Mr. Carillo," she said, and tried to step around him. Louis Carillo, the heavy gambler, was one person she wanted to stay clear of.

But he blocked her path. "I've heard the good news. The news about you and Whirlwind. Mr. Blair is a smart man. Only a smart man would hire one of the best up-and-coming jockeys on the East Coast."

"If you'll excuse me, Mr. Carillo . . ."

Carillo put out his huge hand and took hold of Carmen's right arm. He pulled her toward him. "I have some news for you, my dear. I have bet a lot of money on the Sullivan Stakes tomorrow—all of it on Fast Dancer to win."

Carmen started to say something, but Carillo wouldn't let her.

"No, don't say anything. Not yet. Let me finish what I have to say to you first."

Carmen nodded and said nothing.

"When I bet on a race, I always bet on a sure thing. Now, in the case of the race tomorrow, I believe that Fast Dancer and his jockey, Billy Crane, *are* a sure thing."

"I don't want to talk about the race, Mr. Carillo."

Carillo's hand tightened on Carmen's arm, almost hurting her. "You don't have to talk about the race—just *listen*—understand."

Carmen tried to break away from Carillo. She couldn't.

"Let me go!" she said.

Carillo didn't let Carmen go. Instead he put his left hand into his pocket. "No other horse in tomorrow's race can come close to beating Fast Dancer—except Whirlwind. He might win with you riding him. But that must not happen."

Carillo's hand came out of his pocket. There was money in it. "I have here one thousand dollars, my dear. It's all yours.

Just hold Whirlwind back on the final turn, and keep him from winning. When you have done that, I will pay you two thousand more."

"I don't want your money!" Carmen cried.

"Take it!" Carillo said sharply and put it into the pocket of Carmen's jacket, before she could stop him.

"Look at the matter this way, Miss Solar," Carillo said. "There will be many other races in the days to come. I don't care if you win every one of them. But I don't want you to win the Sullivan Stakes. Is that clear?"

Frightened, Carmen could only nod.

And then Carillo let her go, got in his car, and drove away.

That night, sitting in Leo Mendoza's apartment, Carmen was angry—very angry. She looked hard at her boyfriend and said, "I won't throw the race!"

"But you just told me that you were afraid of what Carillo might do, if you crossed him and didn't hold Whirlwind back," he said.

"I don't care!" But Carmen knew she did care. She *was* afraid of what Carillo might do if she crossed him.

"Like Carillo said to you, it's just one race," he said. "No one will ever know that you held Whirlwind back to keep him from winning."

"*I'll* know!" Carmen cried, feeling angry

and sad and worried all at the same time. "Leo . . ." She held his hand. "You know how hard I've worked all these years to become a jockey. Now I am one, and I'm a good one."

"I know you are." Leo leaned over and kissed her. "I know you are a good jockey—one of the best."

Carmen gave him a sad little smile. "What if someone found out that I'd thrown the race? I would be finished as a jockey."

"No one will ever find out. I'm sure they won't." Leo looked down at his hand in Carmen's. "There is our future together to think about. We need money for that. There is your sister to think about. You said you were going to use part of your next winnings to help her pay her hospital bills. You already have the thousand dollars Carillo gave you and . . ."

"I don't want it, not his kind of money. It's dirty money. I would never have taken it from him, but he put it in my pocket before I could stop him."

"You'll have another two thousand dollars of Carillo's money when the race is over. He said so."

Carmen let go of Leo's hand.

"If you come in second or third in the race," Leo went on, "you'll have even more money. Carmen, you don't have to win every race. If you place second or third—with your share of the winnings and Carillo's two thousand dollars, you'll have . . ."

Leo fell silent as Carmen got to her feet and crossed the room. She stood with her back to him, looking out the window.

"So you think I should do what Carillo wants, is that it, Leo?"

"I could take the money you and I have saved together and bet it all on Fast Dancer to win. Carmen, we could make a lot of money that way, just like Carillo is going to do. We can, that is, if you hold Whirlwind back. Like Carillo said to you, it would be like betting on a sure thing."

Carmen felt her whole body stiffen. "A sure thing," she said, echoing Leo. Suddenly, she felt cold. She felt something inside her die. She could not turn and look Leo in the eye. Not now, she couldn't. Maybe not ever again.

"Riders up!"

The words of the racetrack announcer came over the loudspeaker strong and clear. Carmen swung into the saddle, patted Whirlwind on the neck, and rode out onto the track. The other horses and their riders were all around her.

She fought against the fear she was feeling, as she and Whirlwind made their way to the starting gate. When she reached it, Whirlwind went into the gate without any trouble.

Fast Dancer, with Billy Crane aboard, went in right next to them. "Good luck, Carmen," Billy said.

"Good luck to you too, Billy."

"I don't need luck," Billy said, confidently. "Not with a great horse like Fast Dancer, I don't."

Seconds later, a loud bell rang.

"They're off!" the announcer shouted through the loudspeaker.

Whirlwind left the starting gate like a bullet fired from a gun. As the horse raced down the track, Carmen bent low over the animal's neck. She held tightly to the whip in her right hand. She kept her booted feet solidly in the stirrups.

The blue and yellow silks of the Blair stables, that she was wearing, caught the sun and sparkled. The wind was loud in her ears. Whirlwind's mane, whipped by the wind, flew into her face.

Fast Dancer passed her on the right.

Another horse passed her on the left.

As Carmen rode past the sixteenth post, she caught up to the horse on her left and easily passed him. She didn't hear the cheers from the people in the stands. She only heard the clattering of horses' hooves beneath her.

At the three-quarter-mile post, Carmen looked quickly over her shoulder. One horse was only three lengths behind her. But the others were far back on the track.

Turning her head, she rode on. Now, her eyes were on Fast Dancer, nearly five lengths ahead of her. She knew there was still time to catch up to him.

At that moment, Billy Crane looked back over his shoulder. When he saw Whirlwind, he whipped his horse.

Fast Dancer's speed increased. In a

flash, the horse was seven lengths ahead of Whirlwind.

Carmen knew she had to make up her mind—*now*. She thought of all the years she had worked and struggled to become a jockey. And she knew that she couldn't throw all that away. Not for Leo—not for anyone. And certainly not because a man like Louis Carillo had threatened her.

As they came into the final turn, she brought Whirlwind close to the rail. She glanced back once more to make sure she only had one horse to worry about—Fast Dancer. There was nobody behind her for at least eight lengths.

She used her whip on Whirlwind. Once on the right side. Once on the left side.

They gained quickly on Fast Dancer.

The lead had been cut to just two lengths. With less than 50 yards to go, the horses were neck and neck.

Then Whirlwind made one final charge and passed Fast Dancer, as the crowd of 45,000 people roared and cheered.

Carmen stood up and waved the whip after she crossed the finish line. She had won the Sullivan Stakes. There was a big smile on her face as she headed for the winner's circle. She was also holding back tears.

She knew she had done the only thing she could do and stay true to herself. But by doing so, she had lost a lot, too.

The money she and Leo had saved—the money he had bet on Fast Dancer—that didn't matter at all to her. But Leo *did* matter to her and she knew that, because of what he had done, she had lost him too.

When Carmen left the jockeys' dressing room after the race, she was wearing her street clothes. Sam Martin was waiting for her. So was Louis Carillo.

Carmen felt a cold fear at the sight of Carillo, so she moved closer to Sam.

"Your agent," Carillo said to her, "is a smart man."

Carmen wanted to ask Carillo what he meant, but she seemed to have lost her voice.

"Sam Martin is a smart man," Carillo went on, "because he just told me that he bet on Whirlwind to win."

As Carmen looked at Sam, he gave her a big smile.

"And he's not the only smart man around here," Carillo added. "*I* bet on Whirlwind to win, too."

"I'm afraid I don't understand you, Mr. Carillo," Carmen said. "You told me that you were going to bet on Fast Dancer to win. That's why you wanted me to hold Whirlwind back. So that Fast Dancer would be sure to win."

"I told you, my dear," Carillo said, smiling, "that I always bet on a sure thing. I was sure that if I paid you to throw the race, you would do just what you did do. You see, I know what kind of person you are, Miss Solar. I know you are honest. I know you believe in yourself and will do only what you believe is right. I checked you out very carefully before I spoke to you yesterday."

Carmen didn't know what to say. Then she remembered something. She dug into her purse—and came up with the one thousand dollars Carillo had forced on her the day before. She held it out to him.

"Keep it, Miss Solar," he said. "You earned it. You have made me a lot of money because of the way you rode Whirlwind today."

"No, I won't keep it," Carmen said. "I don't approve of you or the way you make your money, Mr. Carillo. I'm happy I won today. But I'm happy for Mr. Blair, who believed in his horse—and in me." Then she put the money in Carillo's hand—this time forcing *him* to take it.

Carillo shrugged his shoulders. "Well, suit yourself," he said. He smiled slightly and walked away.

Carmen turned to Sam. "Thanks for believing in me, Sam. I wish everyone I care for had your faith." She thought of Leo, sadly. She gave Sam a hug and said, "I'll see you tomorrow. Keep getting me those good rides."

As Carmen walked away from Sam, she almost ran into Leo, coming around the corner of the building. He gave her a big smile, and took a stack of bills out of his pocket.

"Is that the money we saved together?" she asked him.

"Yes, it is. But it is much more than that."

Carmen gave him a puzzled look.

"I won almost two thousand dollars on the race," he explained. "I picked the winner."

"You mean that you bet on . . . ?"

"I bet on you and Whirlwind."

"Leo, I . . ."

"I'm sorry I ever thought of asking you to throw the race," he said. "After you left last night, I realized how stupid I was. And I also realized that in the end, there was only one sure thing in the race—*you*."

Carmen almost burst into tears. "I knew

I could only ride to win," she said. "But I was afraid that I'd lost you at the same time."

Leo smiled. "You'll always be a winner, Carmen," he said. "And if I'm smart I'll be sure to stay right by your side—forever."

Carmen threw her arms around Leo and hugged him as hard as she could.

MEDIA CENTER
SANTA ANA HIGH SCHOOL
520 W. Walnut Street
Santa Ana, Calif. 92701